SWEATLESS VICTORY

By Lawrence D. Tribble, Jr.

Copyright © 2014 Lawrence D. Tribble, Jr.

All rights reserved.

ISBN:978-0-692-02727-1

First Edition

Ldtribble.com
Ellenwood, GA
770-666-2613

All scripture quotations unless otherwise indicated, are taken from the Holy Bible: Amplified, King James Version, Good News Translation. Definitions taken from Merriam-Webster Dictionary.

1.Personal Growth and Self-Development 2. Motivational Speaking 3. Life Coaching 4. Spiritual 5. Inspirational

Cover done by Beth Plummer, Photographs by Angelo Byrd , Edited by Jacqueline Easton Chapman, Edited by Mia Strong

SWEATLESS VICTORY

DEDICATION

To my Glow Baby, the young lady I love without measure. You are the apple of my eye; the only thing in my life that I cherish more than myself. Life has a strange way of not going the way we want or even expect. There have been so many days that I have wanted to spend with you; watch you sleep, smile and wipe your tears as they fall. However, due to things out of our control those days have never happened. I have watched you blossom into the young princess I've all ways dreamed you would be. I'm so proud of the beautiful, adorable woman you have grown up to be and I am amazed at the incredible work ethic you possess. You're my angel, my motivation to press on and make you proud to call me dad. I may not be there physically, but there is not a day that passes that you are not in my thoughts or my prayers. You are a part of me no matter how far you are, and no matter how long I don't hear your voice. GOD has an unfathomable plan for your life. The words that I write in this book will hopefully give you direction and inspiration to become all that I know you will become. You are beautiful, intelligent, and full of special zeal for life. I may not know what the future has for you, but I know the Creator that does. Hold on to your faith and BELIEVE that your way is already made. I dedicate this book to you my darling, and I pray that it empowers you to soar higher than I could possibly IMAGINE. You have gifts and talents in you that you must trust and let GOD lead you to the places HE has for you go. Never let me or anyone limit what your inner-voice is telling you to do or be. Your fingerprint is like no others and it should be used to impact the world. Your creativity is bigger than you understand right now, but it will be revealed when it's time. Stay focused and motivated to do whatever your heart desires. I'm proud of you for being just who you are, and no matter what, I will always be your loving father supporting you in every endeavor. Trust your struggles, understanding that it's necessary for your growth. You have everything you need to be the person that GOD has designed you to be. Never give or lose hope because hope is what fuels you for greatness. You are a diamond! You are created to shine brighter than the sun. If there is not a path you want to follow it is because your destiny is to cut out on your own. I have faith that you will bless me and the world with your purpose. Life is about dreaming and allowing those dreams to become a reality. Keep dreaming baby girl and imagining yourself there. Your fight is fixed and is from a position of victory! No matter what you encounter, you have already won with SWEATLESS VICTORY! I LOVE YOU MORE THAN THE AIR I BREATHE AND WILL CARRY YOU THROUGH THE STORM AND THE RAIN IF NECESSARY. As the tears roll up in my eyes with every thought of you, I'm reminded that you're my first born and only child, and I cherish you more than words can describe. I Love you Mariah Martin, signed your loving father!

LAWRENCE D. TRIBBLE, JR.

CONTENTS

Acknowledgments

	PRELUDE	14
1	What's My WHY	18
2	How Do I Get Motivated?	27
3	Do I Need a Mentor?	36
4	Is the Influence of the Media and Reality TV Hurting Me?	46
5	Why Are We So Concerned with What Others Think of Us?	56
6	Why Do We Have Tribulations?	63
7	What do you do While Waiting on Your Manifestation?	70
8	How Do You Conquer Fear?	77
9	How Do you Find PURPOSE?	80
10	How Do You Take Action?	90
11	Affirmations	98
	ABOUT THE AUTHOR	106

ACKNOWLEDGMENTS

First, I would like to acknowledge the King Almighty, the GOD I serve that has been so faithful and gracious unto me, even when I didn't want to listen and follow HIS path which HE set before me. I want to thank the LORD for every trial and tribulation that caused me to seek HIS face even more. "This DIVINE TRANSITON" has been the BIGGEST BLESSING of my life yet, and I'm so humbled that HE chose me. I feel like David in 2 Samuel 7:20-23 in the Amplified version when he said "What more can I say to you? For you know your servant, O LORD GOD. Because of Your Promise and Your own heart dictates, You have done all these astounding things to make Your servant know and understand. Therefore You are great, O LORD GOD; for none is like You, nor is there any GOD besides You, according to all [You have made] our ears to hear". David, like I, was expressing in words the best way to thank and describe this awesome great GOD we serve. I have found that in everything there is a lesson that has been good for my growth. I have learned to look at life from a New Testament prospective. BY GOD'S Grace (unmerited favor) sin is no longer an issue or stronghold. There is no condemnation in Christ Jesus. With this understanding, it has become a lot easier to be who GOD has called me to be, and I find myself falling short less than before. GOD, I'm so grateful for the things you have shown me on this journey, and I make an oath to never return to that superficial, self-centered, stiff-neck believer I turned into. With that said, I would like to apologize to anyone I have ever made feel less than who GOD said you were. I ask my family, my brother Ali Tribble to forgive me for leaving Cincinnati and turning my back on you. You have been my rock in this DIVINE TRANSITION, I love you dearly. That goes for my youngest brother Lance Chapman and Lonel Tribble as well; I apologize for not building the necessary relationship with you when I left the city. Donte Tribble, thanks for letting GOD use you cousin, love you as well. Now to my beautiful Mother (Jacqueline Chapman), I'm at a loss for words when it comes to you. We have been through so much as mother and son that I don't know where to start. You were the first woman I have ever loved and you have truly shown me what type of woman I need in my life. You raised me to fear and reverence the GOD I served, and have led by example. You have not been a perfect mother, nor have I been a perfect son. I have always known that you loved me, and that our dedication to the mission of GOD has sometimes clouded our view on the real importance of living. During this journey, you have been the mother I have always wanted as a small child. You have been a shoulder to cry on when others have hurt me, you have taken your little and sacrificed for me, and you have been a voice in the wilderness that I have learned to trust and depend on in times of need. You have become my best friend and number one confidante. I will love you for the rest of my life. Thank you mommy. Mathew B Coleman, the bible says there is a friend that sticks closer than a brother, and that my friend, has been you. You have been a true friend; always supporting me, even when I didn't know it. Even though we fought a lot in the beginning of this TRANSITION, it was all out of love and support, pushing each other to become our best. For that, Brother Malcolm (LOL), I love and appreciate you for being someone I could take the mask off with and be myself. You will never be forgotten or devalued.

Jo Queen Coleman, what a GOD send. Queen, I tell you all the time, but I'm telling you now for the world to know what you mean to me. I thank GOD every day for using you to open my eyes to a whole other lifestyle. GOD is a SPIRIT and has to use people to get HIS will done. Thank you for being that vessel. You have made so many things possible for me, from exotic islands in the Caribbean, to the Four Seasons Hotel Los Angeles in Beverly Hills. You are an amazing, generous woman and I cannot wait to see the blessings you reap for all that you do for so many; the organizer, supporter, and peacemaker. You have so many wonderful talents and gifts that have made many love you, as I do. Thank you again for being just who you are. Love you to life!

Latanya Wimberly, what a blessing you have been! Thank you for your love, support, and acts of kindness. You have encouraged me tremendously through your words and the financial seeds you have sown during my time of need. If no one has ever believed in me, I know you have. The love I have for you will never change, thank you.

Neil Harris, I want to thank you for opening up your home to me for 8 long months and never asking me for one dime while being a guest in your home. There are not many people out here who would ever be so gracious. For that, I declare and decree GOD'S Blessing on your life according to Genesis 12:3 "And I will Bless those who Bless you" [who confer prosperity or happiness upon you].

Shelly Slough, my God sister, what a friend you have been for close to 17 years. You have supported every vision I've ever had and have backed it with your time, energy, and finances. This book would not even be possible without your encouragement that kept pushing me to write more and more. You're a GOD-sent and life-long friend that I will always cherish and love with the love of Christ. Thank You Shell, Shell..!

Mia Strong, you have been such a friend when excellence was needed. From helping me with my professionalism with my web page to the editing of this book. Thank for honoring what you heard GOD say, concerning being a tremendous support and key person to the success of this book. With school, work, and your everyday life raising your son, you found time to believe in me and offered your skills set and made this book possible. Thank you for helping me self-publish. Love you dear friend for all you have done.

I want to thank my current Pastors of 8 months, Creflo & Taffi Dollar, for their dynamic teaching and covering me during my TRANSITION to Atlanta, Ga. I feel like I have been in school for these few months. It was definitely ordained for me to sit under your ministry for such a time as this. I have learned so much in such a short time. It's amazing. I love your leadership and the transparency you Pastor in. I will continue to be a faithful member until GOD call's me elsewhere. Last, but definitely not least, my Spiritual Mother of 12 years Dr. Patricia P. McKinstry. What a strong beautiful women of GOD you are, inside and out. You have truly been Jesus on earth to me. I have learned so much from you even before I became a member of your church December 31, 2001. I watched your faithfulness to your Spiritual Leader, my then Pastor, the late Honorable Bishop William Morgan James. I watch how you reverenced the GOD in him, and how you supported and protected him. You didn't know me then but you were teaching me how to honor leadership. Like the great Bishop James, you continued to teach me the WORD OF GOD with no compromise. If it weren't for your transparency as a true leader and your incredible support that you have given me, spiritually and financially, as well as serving as an example, this TRANSITION could not have been possible for me. You have praised me when I was doing well and chastised me when I wasn't doing my best. You saw and spoke greatness into my life, and for all of that I want to thank you with my whole heart for being that GODLY vessel in my life that GOD has used to inspire me to follow my purpose to destiny. Those that don't know this dynamic women of GOD, you need to find her. She pastors the Worship Center, 2204 Collingwood BLVD, Toledo, Ohio 43620 (419) 244-2100. There have been a host of people that have supported me financially, emotionally, and spiritually on this journey, but for the sake of not creating another whole chapter, I must refrain from mentioning every ones names, but you know who you are.

Thank you for believing in me and supporting me! Stay tuned for my next GOD inspired book, Love you all with the love of Christ Jesus…!!!

2Chronicles 33: 12 Amplified. "When I was in affliction, I besought the Lord my GOD and humbled myself greatly before the GOD of my fathers"

PRELUDE

Transition is described as a movement, development, or evolution from one form, stage, or style to another. This book is about one man's Faith walk to purpose and the hidden treasures that were found through the obedience to his inner-voice (GOD). This book will serve as a true example of how the Universe will open up when you starve your fears and feed your faith and when you have more faith in GOD'S promises than you have in the lies of this world. Go on a journey with me as I transition and share with you some of my intimate thoughts while fighting through trials, tribulations, heart break, and the everyday frustrations of life. Through this journey, you will get a chance to visualize how I battled between following the principles of this worldly system as opposed to following the principles of GOD'S Kingdom. Witness my growth and how I learned what it was to become a "True Believer in Christ Jesus" and the cross one must bear to walk in His promises. Obedience allowed me not to make any excuses for my situation and empowered me to follow that inner-voice to freedom.

As believers, it is by faith that you must launch out into all the possibilities that the finished works of Jesus offer us. Take a trip with me as the Lord allowed me to be broken, pruned, and developed through heartache, deception, and my own carnal(selfish) desires. Find out how dating some of the most beautiful women men would ever want, still brought me no true self-worth, and only served as a reminder of what popularity and material attracts from people. Read how with zero income I received a peace that surpassed all natural understanding, which produced a life of substance and passion for the things of GOD. Find out how I learned that a certain picture you paint of yourself will cause others to love you with a worldly love (emotional); love that is based on the possibilities of what could be, not the God kind of love, which is committed love; meaning circumstances can't change it.

Through this spiritual journey, GOD showed me what true substance looks like and how important our design, purpose, and our WHY for living is. Without purpose, life is as shallow as a person dating because of status or the type of car someone drives. The sad reality is that this is what America is turning into; a bunch of people chasing people and things (myths) for happiness; their made up answer to completeness.

I was inspired to write this book to help guide and save our next generation of young people and possibly give revelation to my peers and elders.

Before this transition, I thought I was living a life of selflessness and dedication to helping the plight of mankind by fostering homeless children and providing many different services and programs for uneducated and economically challenged families in my city. Through this transition however, GOD has shown me that this was all vain works and that I haven't even scratched the surface of servitude. You are only as good as the people you help to realize the potential and purpose that they possess. You must pour yourselves out completely to help the lost, and let the LORD refill you.

This Transition has opened my eyes to a whole other realm of possibilities in which I want to share with the world. It has shown me a world where material and money are just things that SERVE us and not what we serve. During this transition, I have learned how to live in a different government; the government of the Kingdom of GOD, a debt free system of doing things. Read and find out how to be translated into a new system of living that's not controlled by wants (greed, and selfish desires), but by purposeful GOD directed living. People that are after the riches of this world will never really experience the Joy of the LORD, which is our true strength and completeness.

By the end of this book you will feel empowered. No longer will you accept the lies your circumstances tell you. You will learn to appreciate the small things in life and understand that walking by faith may entail being broken from of all your desires and selfish wants. You may be forced to trust your struggle with your heart broken from bad relationships or just everyday situations, and all the while doing the will of GOD for your life, while waiting on HIS promises to manifest. After reading this book, my prayer is that you start to challenge yourself to ask GOD to enlighten your eyes of understanding and form an ear to hear HIS voice (that inner voice). Be blessed my friends and stay tuned to my next GOD inspired book…I love you with the Love of Christ our LORD and SAVIOR..!!!

1

WHAT'S MY WHY?

We as people have an innate capacity to dream and yearn for the things in our heart, yet rarely do we achieve those things. As a child, these visions were very real and attainable, but as adolescence and adulthood set in, that passion for the things we saw ourselves achieving and becoming, somehow lost their way.

Years prior, there was no limit to the things we could believe and ask for. In our minds, we could build skyscrapers and take trips to outer space. Our minds were shaped from the cartoons we watched and the fairytale books we read. The adults around us would reinforce those ideas and dreams. They would say things like "You can do whatever you set your mind to do". It didn't matter how outlandish it may have sounded. It was always an adult somewhere that would agree with whatever vision we had. We were practicing auto suggestion (self-talk) without even knowing it, everywhere we went and with everyone we came in contact with. The postman would know our vision, along with our teachers, pediatricians, family members and even strangers as we traveled through our everyday functions of life. Back then, it seemed as though everyone we were around agreed with our desires to fly to heights unknown and our thoughts of launching out into uncharted waters. The people surrounding us seemed to reinforce and agree with us to becoming doctors, judges, and extraordinary inventors. Somewhere, somehow, in transition from adolescence to adulthood, those dreams and visions got lost. What happened? Did we just grow up and decide that those thoughts where just foolish behavior? Did someone tell us that those dreams and visions were impossible to achieve? What happened to those people that believed in us? Why did we stop giving ourselves permission to think outside the paradigm of what we see in our now.

On the path to finding your WHY, these questions must be explored, examined, and answered. These answers are the keys to unlock those doors. The closer we get to our WHY, the more it becomes your true reason for living. Your WHY is found in the testing of every lesson learned along the way. Out of these lessons, we move closer to our dreams and visions.

Opposition causes desperation; desperation births character and your true promise. Your true promise is what your character shows you during these times. Martin Luther King Jr. stated "The ultimate measure of a man is not where he stands in moments of comfort and convenience, but where he stands in times of challenge and controversy" (desperation). This quote reminds me of a man in the bible named Joseph. Joseph was considered a dreamer by his family. I would dare to say he wasn't just a dreamer, but a visionary. I say visionary because his brothers spoke of him as if he was stuck in some type of fantasy land. Like someone lost in a world of make believe. Even his dad was taken aback by Joseph's dream. Joseph was surrounded by people that didn't support his vision. His brothers hated him because their father favored him, and his father chastised him for speaking the things he saw in his dreams.

I would like to stop for a moment and break down what happened here. This happens every day in households around the world. There are always going to be people that won't believe in the dreams and visions GOD has designed for your life. In this case it was family, which in most cases causes a deeper hurt. We are taught that blood is thicker than water, and that family sticks together no matter what the circumstances. Our family is usually our first point of reference, but unfortunately can be the same set of people who introduce us to opposition. In some cases, as young as 5 years old, we have negative, abusive affirmations spoken over and to children everywhere. I see it in the grocery store, at the bus stop, and even in church...yikes!

Yes even in the house of GOD. What do you think that's doing to that child? That impressionable child who is looking at the world for the first time, through a brand new pair of eyes and sees no limits to what he or she can do in it. Then here comes some insecure, lazy, dream killer, who's been hurt through bad choices they have made in life or who has never recouped from the abuse that has infected them. This person now wants to warn everyone else about how bad life is and that no matter how hard you work and try to better yourself, life has a way of letting you down. They make comments like; "save yourself the trouble and don't expect good things to happen to you, cause they won't" or "the bad always outweighs the good". This person is usually grumpy and will always magnify the negatives in any given topic. This could be a brother, sister, or mother and father, GOD forbid. Unfortunately this situation happens way too often, and causes dreams and visions to be lost all over the world. This is a very serious epidemic that is destroying generations of people. I say destroy, because identity and purpose are locked up in the dreams and visions you have.

When identity and purpose are lost, life has no meaning. Your WHY is choked out and falls to the wayside. To have vision, you must first have a dream. Dreaming is the beginning of a vision. The simple fact that you dream doesn't mean you are a visionary however. Being a visionary, means you have the courage to walk that dream out. Many people have dreams or had dreams, but have never muscled up the strength to walk those dreams out. Maybe just like Joseph, you have had dream killers in your family that have put out your flame. Dreams give life, so when an individual tries to smother your dreams, in a sense, they're trying to kill you. Sounds harsh I know, but there is a lot of truth to that.

If you lose sight of what you were created to do, your identity is compromised and others are affected as well. Did you know that what we do and don't do have a direct or indirect impact on others around us?

Joseph's brothers sought out to kill him and covered it up by lying to their father about how it happened. If it were not for one of his brothers suggesting to just throw him in a pit, they may have murdered their own brother which would have had a direct impact on the entire planet. After throwing him in a pit, they ended up selling Joseph to some merchants. Joseph was sold into slavery! Can you imagine that? Sold by your family because of your amazing dream (vision), and the fact that you were favored by your father. Joseph had two options at this point. #1 he could scream, fuss, and cuss about his new found situation and complain about how unfair life was treating him or #2 he could choose to make the best of where he was at and trust the process in his transition from dreaming to becoming. What Joseph was quickly finding out, is that for a dream to be manifested, there is a price one must pay to achieve their WHY for being. There are some people you must leave behind; some loved ones you may have to sacrifice for the experience that is necessary to walk out your vision.

Pursuing your why takes courage, a will to succeed, and persevering through whatever opposes you. Joseph accepted his challenges as a servant in another man's house. He had to believe that this was just training ground for the vision to come to pass. I say this because Joseph did such a good job. According to the story, the man trusted him to have charge over his entire household, and even left him alone with his wife. That's incredible trust for a servant. The story doesn't end there however. One day, while his master was away, his wife tried to lure Joseph into her bed. Joseph, being a man of integrity, didn't want to betray his master and ran. The master's wife was so humiliated at the fact that Joseph wouldn't sleep with her, that she changed the facts of what transpired. She told her husband that Joseph tried having his way with her. Her husband was so furious and saddened with betrayal that he had Joseph arrested and thrown into prison. Now here is Joseph locked up in prison for a crime he did not commit. What's going through his mind now? Could he be thinking his life is over? Is he yelling and screaming about how unfair life has been, or maybe how evil the people in his life have treated him? The story never made reference to Joseph doing any of those things, only maintaining his integrity and operating in his gifts. After being imprisoned, it wasn't long after when Joseph was promoted to being the head overseer of the prison. How could someone that has had so much tribulation in their life stay so focused and continue to be committed to someone else's life? It's called understanding your WHY for existing. Joseph knew that he was destined for greatness, and because GOD was with him, he prospered. (Gen 39:2).

When you have vision, temporary distress and let downs become something you can handle. The fuel for stamina is your WHY. Your WHY will produce hope and hope will afford you the endurance to persevere the challenges of life.

So how do you find your WHY? Joseph's life never lost meaning because he had vision; a WHY. From a dream he gave birth to destiny. As Joseph continued to operate in his gifts and talents (interpreting dreams), his gift eventually put him in the company of the Pharaoh in Egypt. The Pharaoh needed an answer to a dream that had been troubling him. One of the men who was in prison with Joseph, told the Pharaoh about a man that had interpreted his dream two years prior. This man happened to be Joseph. Just like the man said, Joseph interpreted the Pharaoh's dreams and saved the country from starvation. The Pharaoh was so impressed with Joseph's gifts that he put him second in charge, under him alone, for the entire kingdom. This position ended up being the authority that caused his dream as a little boy to come to pass. Eventually, his brothers and father had to bow before him, like he saw in his dream. Joseph found his WHY, and it started with a dream that empowered him not to give up, and blame others for defeat. He walked his dream out, into a vision that inspired him. Joseph was motivated because he believed in his dreams, which continued to give his life meaning, regardless of the obstacles he faced.

As you trust the storms of life, be courageous enough to follow your dreams into self-realization; your WHY. Life challenges and tribulations started to become "sweatless" victories, filled with lessons learned and talents developed. Joseph never showed fear, and stayed in positive thought, which allowed him to have clear reasoning when every trial came. To find your WHY in life, you have to win private victories with yourself. You have to be able to tell yourself consistently that you are a winner and align your lifestyle with that belief.

Finding your WHY, might mean you will have to

do the un-popular things in life and travel the road least traveled. It amazes me how so many people follow the crowd when GOD was very intentional and distinctive in the differences between every individual. Why would every person that has ever been born have a different finger print? What would be the purpose of having different hair follicles? Don't you think GOD had some type of plan for creating us similarly yet different?

Every one of us has a unique and special meaning they bring to the world, our WHY for being. I also believe that everything you need in order to connect with that WHY, is already in you. You just have to be courageous enough to walk that thing out. Believe in your dreams and become that man or woman of vision that you have been called to be. Start believing in the purpose that lies within by focusing on those gifts and talents you have been afforded. Living in this consciousness, while daily renewing your mind with positive affirmations that assert where you want to go in life, and your WHY for being will become not just something you wish for, but a daily experience with an expected plan.

2

HOW DO I GET MOTIVATED?

MOTIVATION is described as the process that initiates, guides, and maintains goal-oriented behavior. What causes one to act, whether it is getting a glass of water to reduce thirst, or reading a book to gain knowledge.

There are two types of MOTIVATION. Extrinsic, is an outside motivation to win something like a prize or to refrain from a consequence. Think about the motivation a high school athlete may have to perform, in hopes of being accepted to the college of his or her choice. That is an outside motivation (extrinsic). Motivation that comes from the inside because of some personal gain is intrinsic. This is an internal desire to do something without looking to be rewarded from any outside source. We all know someone who is only motivated by external recognition. These people constantly need rewards to feel important. They cannot function without their ego being stroked. Whether your motivation stems from an extrinsic or intrinsic source, we all have something that will motivate us. Some seek motivation through money, fame, notoriety, and even religion.

I have come to understand, that without possessing motivation that comes from within, life becomes one big letdown after the other. There won't always be a reward for things we as constructive citizens are called to do in life. Some things we just have to do because it is the right thing to do. It is a known fact that we can do the right things for the wrong reasons or because of the wrong motivation. Think about how wrong it would be to expect some type of external reward for proper parenting. How wrong would it be to expect to be given praise from friends and family based off of how great you provide and encourage your kids to succeed in life. Even though praise sometimes comes along with being a good parent, it would be ludicrous for that to be your motivation.

    Let's get less personal. Let's say you're a police officer whose job is to protect and serve. However, you never get a reward or a pat on the back for keeping the community safe, or some special ribbon for service rendered. That should not be your only motivation for serving the community. That type of motivation only, would be wrong and frowned upon. Certain things in life should be motivated from the love, passion, and reward you get on the inside for your services. It keeps the integrity in tack.

So what happens if you can't seem to be motivated by anything? If this is something that you have issues with, it could be a sure indication that you are struggling with purpose and identity. I will be touching on purpose in a later chapter. If you suffer from the lack of the right types of motivation, there are several things that may give you that push you're looking for. Somewhere along the line, you have probably been unappreciated or taken for granted and have lost your zeal for life, which has stifled your passion. Passion is the common denominator for motivation. It increases your motivation and makes the impossible, possible. Passion will motivate you to do things without attaching any monetary value to it. Passion has motivated me to start several organizations over the years.

It started first by volunteering my time and efforts at different schools, as well as to help build community outreach projects. Starting about 18 years ago, when I finished college, I had no motivation to do anything else but play football. As football ended for me, I realized quickly that if I did not get motivated soon, I would slowly start to die internally with no sense of belonging. My reality was that the last 8 years of my life was dominated and consumed by my dreams of playing football in college and the NFL. This had been my WHY for living as long as I could remember. So now that football was over, I had lost my motivation. I had no idea what else I was good at and had never explored any other possibilities. I had never been a part of any social clubs or had a real job. I felt lost and without purpose. One day I was given a book by a mentor, now life-long friend. This book was the first of hundreds of books I would later invest in. I love to read because books give you the ability to escape your now reality. Books will allow you to dream as big and wide as you can possibly imagine. The book that I was given to read talked about the importance of purpose, and directed me to explore things that I forgot I had an interest in.

After completing this book, I decided to take action. I wanted to volunteer my knowledge of track and field at a local school. This was the best decision I have ever made at this stage of my life because it set the stage of development for so many other opportunities that I did not know were possible. Being a state contending athlete in track & field during my high school years, gave me a certain passion for the sport. Helping coach these young students brought back so much excitement and overwhelming joy. I felt as though I was actually competing again. Who would have thought that volunteering my time would ever be so rewarding? For the first time since playing football, I was now motivated to do something else. After that first season, I was offered a paid position to coach. What an unexpected surprise. As I started coaching and becoming more acquainted with the youth. I developed such a love; not just for coaching, but for helping these young men develop into productive citizens and future leaders in our community. By coaching, I was motivated to be a part of the solution to many of the problems I saw hindering the development of the youth I coached. What I saw was a need for African American men in the school system. With the teachers being predominately white females, I saw a huge opportunity for me to be a major, motivating factor. I realized quickly, that most of the boys were developing an immediate bond with me partly because I was male, and also because I was African American. These kids struggled with identity issues. A lot of these boys were from single family homes and did not have any relationship with their fathers. Even worse, some did not know their fathers at all. I found myself having several life talks with these young men. They were clueless for the most part, of who they were and where their place was in the world. This made school not to be a true place of importance. This meant they didn't have a true WHY for coming to school. What did school mean for their future? Most were not sure. Through the many conversations I consistently had with these youth, they felt that most of their other teachers could not relate because of gender and color. This was a 99% black school, with 95% white teachers. I learned quite a bit over those two years of coaching and teaching. The number one thing I learned was the need for African American men in the school system, and what that did for the black boys.

This motivated me even more to find other ways to make a greater impact on the overall growth and refinement of those young men. My passion pushed me to start an organization that would cater to at-risk boys. During the development stages, I was asked by a good friend of mine from college, Kevin Coburn, to be a part of an organization that he helped to found. This organization catered to the same population of youth I was working with. His program focused on intervention-prevention for foster kids. I accepted the job and learned so much about the social service world, which was much of the information I needed to build my organization. I worked for this organization for two years before I was able to start my company. There were many days I wanted to give up on the dream that became my WHY for being because it just seemed so far away. I kept speaking positive affirmations concerning where I saw myself being in six months up to one year. Even though I loved mentoring, providing direction, and supporting foster parents in my program, I knew it was much more I could do with the vision GOD had given me.

September 1, 2001 I finally opened my door for business, after four and a half years of preparing. The Her-em-Ahket Boys Academy was finally a reality. After many tears, long hours of preparation, and a house gifted to me by the late Bishops William Morgan James, I received my first client. On the day our country was attacked by terrorist, I was stepping into my promise. What if I would not have read that book? What if I had not gotten motivated to go and volunteer at Toledo Scott High School? Where would I be now? These are questions I don't have to answer because I did read the book, and it did motivate me to volunteer. It did motivate me to teach, and to take action on the new dreams that were passionately planted in my heart, as I continued to accept my WHY for existing. Please don't think this was an easy task because it wasn't. I had many frustrations and down moments on this journey. For one, I had to change my circle of influence. I was no longer hanging out with the "fellas" and watching the "idiot box" (television). These are the number one things that can make or break you. The people you associate with the most, impact your decision making. The information you take in through media, television, as well as the music you listen to, will have a direct influence on the way you think. This intake of information also shapes the way you look at life and the things that govern it.

I developed a new circle of influential, concerned, individuals that spoke purpose into me and helped guide me through the process of life. The same thing I was offering the kids was being given to me. The first, was my mentor and Godfather Derrick E. Roberts. He was the man who gave me the book to read, along with his continual support. Willie Ann Moore (Momma Moore) encouraged me continuously with words of vision. Momma Moore would talk to me about my potential as a young teacher. She would always tell me that I was bigger than where I was at and that I should be on a bigger stage, so the world could see my gifting. As a 23 year old young man struggling with direction, this was so very special to me. This was motivation on another level. Not only did I want to succeed for me, but now I had other people rooting for me. Years prior my good friend Kevin Coburn, saw my gifts and talents way beyond my initial enlightenment.

Motivation comes from taking risks, learning something new, and trusting the unknown. Life has a funny way of directing you down the right path to follow, when you surround yourself with positive people, that have what you want out of life; people that are passionate about your success and future. There are people that have the ability to pull the best out of you, but don't be fooled because there are also people that possess the ability to pull out the worst in you.

Prioritizing plays a very significant role in becoming motivated. Your quality of life starts to change from a person unmotivated to a person that takes action. It saves you from wasting your time and efforts on contrary and futile involvements. Prioritizing and being motivated go hand in hand because they both will define you, once they are put into action. Prioritizing, is putting first things first and having a focal point, and a systematic approach of doing things. It's something about having a calculated focus on something that gives you better clarity of thought; a certain will power, that will help you line up resources that creates goals with a specific intent. Boundaries are set when you prioritize. So many times we have good intentions, but take on too much, which leads to stress, loss of focus and ineffectiveness. People that prioritize understand that they may have to give up some opportunities to honor their commitment to the priorities they have set for themselves. I'm not saying you can't ever deviate from the set plans or routine you have put in motion, because there is always room for change, but prioritizing helps you stay on course in your invisible lane.

3

DO I NEED A MENTOR?

When you are in search of purpose and destiny, you must continually transform in order to become bigger and better. Now the question becomes "what do you do to become bigger and better?" If you knew that answer, you would already be where you wanted to go and there would be no reason for transformation. Transformation happens by the information received throughout life's journey. Everything we need to know is learned in this journey. You just have to find the road map. This road map allows you to get to the destination designed for you. Each person has a different destination, but similar paths or trails. Those that believe in their dreams and know their WHY for living, increase their capacity of growth by investing their time and efforts listening to a mentor.

Mentors are usually older than the person they are mentoring, but not 100% of the time. They are considered wise or more experienced because they have already traveled the roads ahead of you. Mentors understand that the true design of struggle is to accelerate your life. Mentors are problem fixers and enlighteners. They help you to see the invisible, by equipping, strengthening, and assisting.

Our potential is maximized when we connect with others that know how to empower. Once you are empowered, you become armed to find that authentic self. I have had several mentors on this journey, and when I think about the ultimate mentor, I think of Jesus Christ. Jesus was not just a prophet and GOD in the flesh, but a supreme leader that embodied mentorship. He discipled men and gave perfect guidance. Jesus would ask deep, insightful questions that would serve to not only teach, but allowed his disciples to search for their own answers. He even mentored through chastisement (discipline), knowing that is the only way some people learn at times. How many times growing up have we had to be chastised by a parent to get true understanding? Even at the workplace there is chastisement used to educate (mentor) and keep staff within certain boundaries. Mentorship is the catalyst that jump-starts and pushes us to the next level.

How do you find a mentor? Well your first mentor usually finds you. Your first mentor may very well be mom, dad, a family member, or a coach. Our parents were designed to be the first people that lead, chastise, and empower us. They teach through their verbals and non-verbals. Some of us even start to walk and talk like our parents. Our first understanding of the world and the people in it comes from what our parents teach us. They teach us how to treat others, along with what is proper and improper. Your first pep talk, preparing to hit that ball off the tee in your first little league baseball game, came from mom and or dad. Who counseled you through your first heartbreak, and helped you to move forward? If your parents were anything like my parents, you had a whole laundry list of things you learned and emulated years after you left there tutelage. Mentors leave a stamp of influence that continues to lead and guide, years after they're no longer around. You never outgrow mentorship. Life is about forward progress. As long as you're living, you should be aspiring to expand your knowledge and the impact you have in this world. The mark you leave here in this world is extremely important. I repeat, everyone has a purpose; a designed goal and task they were created to accomplish. I truly believe there would be a cure for HIV, cancer, and even the common cold if everyone would function in their purpose. Mentors help us find direction and build upon gifts and talents. Every person that has achieved any level of success, has had mentors. Mentors help speed up the process of achieving. Have you ever heard someone say, "don't reinvent the wheel"? This term simply means, not to spend time doing something that has already been done. The forest has already been cut down, why focus time and attention on how to figure out how to do something that has already been done? Mentors give road maps, and short-cuts to destinations unknown; not just for preparing to work a job either. Mentors are important in every facet and walk of life. I have had had mentors in athletics, social services, and even when I became a believer in Christ. In every vocation and or occupation, whether it's physical or mental, there should be something that sets you apart from everyone else in the universe.

Athletics, is where I first learned the importance of a mentor. As my body was developing, I would watch other athletes that played my desired position and study how they planted their feet to make certain moves and what techniques helped give them a certain edge. I would also ask questions from older athletes that had already reached certain levels of success. These people served as mentors, and helped me develop my skills set from average to playing above average. Things that would have taken me a few more years to learn, I learned in one and two seasons. When I graduated from high school, the level of competition changed dramatically and it was time for new mentors to help teach me what to expect on the collegiate level. In every walk of life, mentors are needed to help even or balance the playing field and make room for hidden potential.

How much untapped potential has been lost or has fallen to the wayside, because of the absence of positive mentors? Thirty-three percent of all first year students drop out of college, due to the lack of direction and failure to properly prioritize. It is a statistical fact that college kids are a lot more likely to graduate after becoming a part of some type of social group. The reason being is that there is a certain level of accountability demanded from the older students that are part of the group. This is a form of positive peer pressure and mentorship. I will never forget how Kevin Coburn, a now close friend, served as a mentor to me my sophomore year of college. Kevin gave me all the ends and outs of how to navigate my way through campus and what resources were available to me. Being a collegiate athlete, I was already afforded a little more support because I was a part of a team. We would hold each other accountable for getting to practice, class, and participating in different study tables. This was a tremendous help in regards to registering for classes and keeping my grades up to par, but didn't scratch the surface of the everyday social pressures of a 19 year old college athlete.

I was not the model student athlete and I was eventually released from the team because of my poor behavior. This leads me to another reason positive mentors are important. After being released from the team, I was officially at an all-time low. My only reason for going to college was to play football, and it was now taken away from me because of self-imposed behaviors. With only one year of school left, I had a serious dilemma. What was my next move? My WHY for being was now taken away. Where would the motivation come from to finish my degree? I didn't have any other skill set I knew about other than athletics and I had no other ambitions. College was all about football and partying. Then one day, as I was walking through the Student Union, I was asked to speak at a forum by none other than Kevin Coburn. I had never laughed so hard in my life. I really thought he had lost his mind to ask someone like me; a guy that had been so mischievous and notorious on campus for doing a little bit of everything. After that moment, there wasn't a day that went by that I didn't think about why he had asked me to speak. I finally developed the nerve to ask him after weeks of straining my brain. The answer he gave me became my new WHY for being.

Before this moment, I could not remember any adult male ever seeing anything great or positive in me aside from athletics. I had always esteemed Kevin as an intellectual who had incredible insight on societal issues. Him telling me what he saw in me and the impact he saw me having on others was a major turning point in my life. Never did I think we would end up fighting social injustices together in our community and helping change the climate in economically challenged areas. We have worked side-by-side mentoring and fathering hundreds of youth that otherwise would have been lost in the concrete jungles of their communities. Since then, I have been a school teacher, track coach, and mentor for Big Brothers & Sisters of America and Treatment Foster Parents for Orphan children. I have ran intervention prevention programs and started two organizations. One was a non-profit called Her-em-ahket Boy's Academy (group home), that housed and nurtured young boys from 8-18 years of age, who were suffering from severe juvenile delinquencies along with neglect and abuse. The second was an intervention/prevention program which is still in operation today, is the Village 50.

The Village 50 is an organization I founded with two other men with similar backgrounds (Albert Earl & Matthew Coleman). Our mission was to bring at least 50 professional minority men together for the sole purpose of mentoring other young men who were not afforded the privilege of having positive, productive males in their lives.

Let's back up for a moment and ask that question again. Do I need a mentor? In my experience, it is imperative and almost impossible to ever reach or even understand your potential, without some form of guidance. As you can see throughout my life, sometimes we cannot pick and choose who we want to mentor us. It just happens when you allow it to take its proper place. Kevin was my peer just a few years older but he was wiser than me and he knew something I did not, which served to be a guide- that light at the end of a dark tunnel; a mentor. After acknowledging your need for a mentor, it becomes easier to detect and understand why you need one. At that point you become more deliberate on who you want as a mentor. I have had several mentors over the years that have helped me to navigate through life's pitfalls as well as mountaintop experiences. I have had financial, relational, and character building mentors. Whatever you find yourself becoming involved in, you will find a need for guidance. When we stop learning and trying to be the best we can be, we fail ourselves.

Nothing blesses me more than to see elderly people still learning and asking questions on how to grow. I truly believe that we can learn from anyone if we are open to really understanding a thing. The children I work with in different capacities, mentor me all the time on the do's and don'ts of adult vs. child behaviors. I have learned which dances should be strictly prohibited for adults to attempt while in the company of children. I have also learned what lingo is only for their peer group. It may sound a little comical, but if not learned, could really make a difference in having a major impact on that child's life. It could be the difference between that child truly being able to feel like you have a clue and that you are worth investing their feelings into.

Learn to step out of your world for a second and be guided by someone else who is going in a direction that you are aspiring to go in or who motivates you to be a better you. I have had friends to tell me that I inspire them by the way I handle disagreements. Even that is a form of mentorship. On the other hand, I have also had people tell me they don't like my vocal tones when I'm passionate about something in conversation, because it comes off to strong and forceful, something they have noticed themselves doing and has not given them the best results.

Life is about choices and arriving at your individual places of destiny. How fast you get there and if you ever make it there at all, will strongly depend on how bad you want to succeed.

Proper mentorship can take you from good to great, and from invisible to visible. You will stop just doing good things, but right things. Good things at the wrong time or season, could serve to be wrong things. Mentors help you learn to make right choices at the right time. I know people that have given their children whatever they ask for with the attitude that they're doing good by their children. Though it may be a good gesture and a nice expression of your love, care and concern, you are doing your child a great disservice! Yes, injustice, injury, and undeserved hurt, have been associated with giving children too much. I have mentored several women over the years who have failed to listen to my wise counsel concerning this matter and later regretted their decisions. The reason that this is not a good practice, is because we are not designed to just receive, but to give. So there must be some form of giving, in order to understand receiving. This has caused this new generation to miss a step. This way of thinking has caused an attitude of self-entitlement. A lot of these young people feel they don't need to be mentored, and that life owes them something.

In the news not too long ago, a young lady was taking her mother to court, to make her pay for her to attend college. When has it been a law for a parent to send their children to college, and pay for it? College is a privilege. This is just one of many examples on why proper mentorship is vital. All of the major leaders and patriarchs have had a guide. That is what our country was founded on; mentors, tutors, and leaders. Whatever you choose to call them, it is in my opinion, that these people are vital to those that choose to be great..

4

IS THE INFLUENCE OF THE MEDIA AND REALITY TV HURTING ME?

Reality shows are like taking small doses of your favorite food infused with poison, that slowly and eventually cause your demise. This type of poison doesn't make you sick however; it only numbs and paralyzes your senses to the realities of your true norms and values. Most people say they understand these facts, yet they still entertain themselves with them. My question is, when did society start being entertained by things that infect the mind with adultery, drugs, and abusive and threatening behavior?

In my opinion, reality TV shows such as these, are rocking you to sleep, and are desensitizing a generation from a value system that founded our country. You want to know what has caused a country that was once the #1 world super power to fall from greatness? It's the infection of morally corrupt television and media influence on a culture.

A person's culture is the intellectual customs they practice. The integrated patterns, beliefs, and behavior. People say; "its only TV," and that they know it's not real, yet it has been proven that whatever you meditate on or are exposed to on a consistent basis, stays lodged in your subconscious. Therefore, when you experience or see the same type of behaviors, those behaviors start to lose their immorality and become familiar (a way of thinking).

After 15 years of fostering homeless and abused children, I saw this first-hand, with the children I worked with. Some of these children associated love with drama. They needed total chaos to feel like things where normal. They would use profanity and abusive behaviors to anger others. Why would a person purposefully create an environment of disharmony? I came to realize, it was because it was something familiar. It was an environment that they had grown accustomed to and considered normal. So in an effort to feel at home or normal, they would try and create that same environment or atmosphere. It was a practice that characterized how they grew up.

Your values, standards, and the things you accept, characterize the culture in which you live. What's really happening when you are being entertained by reality TV is that you are being dummied down to accept the values of what these shows celebrate. In a recent study, it was found that some 63% of the girls that watched reality TV, had a hard time trusting other girls, but only 50% of those who did not watch reality TV had the same thought process. What reality TV is doing is making the abnormal, normal and the normal, abnormal. As you start to absorb the messages in these TV programs, they take root and start to grow inside you. As these ideas grow inside you, they inevitably become a part of you.

The subconscious is a very powerful part of your mind that contains information you can't freely access but functions freely in you. Psychiatrists are still amazed at its function, as they continue to develop new theories and find new developments concerning it. The unconscious mind is the thoughts outside your conscious mind that is developed unconsciously, based on things it has come in contact with. These are memories and desires to do things that you wouldn't consciously do. Have you ever had thoughts to do some really way out things that you could never see yourself doing? Some things you know are not good for you or even lawful? That's your unconscious mind at work, and for this reason it is very important what we feed it. The subconscious mind is a little different because this is information you can access when you direct your attention to it. The subconscious is how you remember directions and places and things you don't have to think about, like using the restroom. You don't have to consciously think about using the restroom, you just go. The problem however, with the subconscious, is that it does not separate fantasy from reality. Your subconscious is what is responsible for emotions during movies and certain reactions to things you may see or read. Even though something is not happening in real life, your subconscious mind perceives it as a real act. Have you ever finished a good Rocky movie and felt like you could be the next boxing champion of the world? Of course you have because your subconscious receives it as a reality and your natural body acts it out. Your brain is the most complex organ in the universe. So much so, that no one knows exactly how it all works factually, just in theory. Researchers do know that the brain processes everything it comes in contact with and downloads it to the memory. Good or bad, it's in there.

As you travel through life, there are billions of deposits made into your mind which will then be processed; the good and bad. That is why four different people can hear the same message and give four different interpretations. One could be a priest who only sees things from a biblical perspective. Another could be a person that has been raised in and out of foster homes their whole childhood, and never really trusted the people raising them due to abuse from their biological parents. The third person could be someone that has been privileged their entire life and has never worked a day. The fourth could be a person with no college degree but has worked extremely hard to survive. All of these people are conscious of the natural laws that govern these United States of America, but due to the fact that their lives are so different, there is a strong possibility that they do not have the same belief system when it relates to morals and values they practice. I am not referring to all cases, but the majority.

I grew up in both rural and the urban areas of Cincinnati, Ohio and there was a tremendous difference in culture. The topics of conversations, standard activities, and communication were almost the complete opposite of each other. In the rural areas I heard more conversations about the freedoms of the world and exploring those opportunities while being responsible, and caring for their children. Parents attended school functions and supported their children. Most of my friend's parents were married, which taught me the importance and value of family. College was stressed consistently, and was understood that attending college went along with succeeding. The years that I spent in the urban areas had a different culture of living. In most cases, values where very different. Survival was the number one attitude. Even the language was different. Conversations were focused more on hustling and getting over on the system. When I say hustling, I'm talking about side jobs to produce other streams of income; legal, but mostly illegal. There was definitely a feeling of oppression and second class citizenship. This culture projected an attitude that only the lucky made it out. College was something that was mostly talked about if you excelled in athletics. Prison on the other hand, was a daily conversation. It was as if we were being groomed for the experience. I saw very few married families. The married families that I did see didn't appear to be very healthy ones. Again, this wasn't everyone, but it was the majority of what I saw and experienced, and the culture I was being grafted into. Even though both sides had their fair share of ignorance, it was safe to say which environment would excel the most with employment opportunities and education. In most cases, based on the cultural differences, these two different cultures will more than likely process what they watch on TV extremely different. Even though they might both agree that it is just TV and may not be appropriate to pattern their lives after, one may find it more appealing to do so, because it fits the actions of the culture they are familiar with.

As a race of people, we are so robotic and consumed with the thoughts of others. This pattern of living starts early at home. It saddens me to see parents who groom their children to out-dress other children, and will allow them to miss school to purchase $200 tennis shoes. These same parents very rarely show up to parent teacher conferences and show no support to their children's progress in school. Most of this behavior stems from media influences as well. I know parents that go out and buy their 9 year-old socks that cost twenty dollars for one pair because some famous basketball star wears them. Is that really a wise investment when you have no savings and you live pay check to pay check? I would say absolutely not, but most people are too consumed with being perceived as a person who has all of their priorities together. The truth is, people would respect you more if you took a stand and stopped following the trends on TV, and being controlled by media influence.

What would happen if you started prioritizing, setting goals, and you had a real plan for your life? I will tell you what would happen. You would start to be led by the things that are inside of you. Those things you were created to do would start to be realized and become priority. Behavior and thoughts like this build true wealth. No longer are you controlled by outside influences that cause regret, fear, stress, and self-esteem issues. Self-worth, identity, and true security are not found in material wealth dictated by the media. Life should be lived as though money were not a consideration. How would you spend your time? What would you value?

In the last year and a half I got the chance to experience that very thing and it has served to be the most liberating, life-changing event in my life. Self-realization is a must for every human being. When you have the opportunity to really tap into the real you, nothing else matters but what your fingerprint offers the world. Every time I would have thoughts about failure and self-pity, I would remind myself that everything I needed, to become who I was called to be, was already inside of me. My Lord and Savior had already paid for my freedom and prosperity. My only job was to believe and walk this thing out without doubt in my heart. Some would say that was a winless battle, that I couldn't start all over in life with a different attitude and mission for my life, and that I couldn't go without a big house, luxury trucks and all the trimmings that came with that type of lifestyle. I'm a living witness that you should trust your inner man, that voice that's telling you to believe in what GOD has already said was yours. Nothing can stop you from reaching destiny. King David was laughed at and mocked for even considering facing Goliath. He wasn't even a solider, but believed the power of his fingerprint. David listened to what was within him, and that was greater than any fear that tried to creep in. Not only did he believe in what GOD had placed in his heart, he fought Goliath with a slingshot and a stone. David took the thing that GOD had been using in him for years to protect his father's sheep, and used it to protect the armies of GOD. David was just one example to show that you have already been given everything you need to win in life, and it may be totally different for you than for anyone else.

You have been uniquely made, a hand crafted vessel that GOD has made in HIS image and likeness. Trust what is in you and let others be inspired to follow you to freedom.

The media is filled with propaganda designed to influence belief in what they're selling. The media's original function was to provide news information on societal issues and to help educate the masses on world affairs. I'm afraid now, that it has shaped the very world we live in. The media was never supposed to shape the minds of our youth and take the place of the moral fibers you live by. They now tell you what to buy and when to buy it. There are billions of dollars spent a year in advertisements that have programed the way the world thinks. This has stunted the growth of America, and has changed the way society thinks.

Let's talk about the obesity issue here in the states that is plaguing our youth. There are millions of adolescents fighting obesity, yet at the same time they are exposed to thousands of advertisements for junk food, and you never see the media advertising overweight, successful people. The people eating the junk food on TV are almost always thin and attractive, which leaves the indication that if you're not thin and attractive on the outside, you will not be successful. This is very dangerous because it paints a vivid picture of how children may view themselves, based on media imagery. Media imagery caters to all five senses. Your visual (seeing), auditory (hearing), kinesthetic (feelings), olfactory (smell), gustatory (taste). Have you ever watched a commercial that made you visualize what the product smelled, tasted, and felt like? The ability to make you receive some form of visual representation is the power of imagery. Am I saying throw away your remotes and give away your televisions? No, but I am saying to be more selective in what you feed your mind. Just like the food you consume, if you don't practice eating healthy, you will eventually pay for it. If you're looking for entertainment to escape the challenges and stresses of your everyday realities. Pick up a good book that stimulates your imagination; a book that inspires you to take action on the things that you have dreamed about as a child. It's never too late to start a new career or take up a new hobby. Start doing healthy things that empower you to feel good about who you are and what is possible for you to achieve in this great world in which you live.

5

WHY ARE WE SO CONCERNED WITH WHAT OTHERS THINK OF US?

Being an athlete afforded me the opportunity to excel in sports. As I excelled in sports, I gained popularity. Athletes and entertainers seemed to be more in demand when it came to popularity. The jocks usually dated the prom queen and had their pick of women they wanted. Over the years, I've pondered why this was so. After years of studying and observing the mind sets of others, it seems to me that perception was the dominate reasoning. I didn't get this revelation until my NFL dreams came to an end and I settled on a career path of educating and driving change in the community where I lived. My first job as a coach and school teacher opened my eyes to this reality. I saw that popular children exhibited higher levels of social competence. They were friendly and more cooperative and engaged readily in conversation. Athletes as a whole, are accustomed to crowds of people cheering and celebrating their efforts and achievements. Through research, I found that youth who play sports seem to earn more money, stay in school longer, and are more engaged in civic life. Athletes also seem to have a bigger edge than students in other activities, such as band, student government, and theater.

Psychologists tend to believe that this is due to the emotional attachment to intense competition, which distinguishes them from other youth. Some even believe that this is where they learn the formula for success. So is it the perception of success that makes athletes popular or is it that people actually respect athletes more? I believe it is because the talents of athletes are showcased more. Repetitive advertisements and what people hear and see the most is unconsciously embedded in their subconscious and makes a person or a situation seem familiar. That is why a class clown or school bully will have his or her fair share of followers as well. Whether your name is being called for doing great things or for mischievous reasons, popularity and influence seem to follow, due to the innate need people have to be validated by those that are relevant in their circle of influence. This is why a major shoe company can pay an athlete millions of dollars to wear (advertise) their shoes.

Perception communicates that if a famous athlete is wearing a certain shoe, then somehow you will become more relevant to your peers if you wear them as well. This kind of thinking starts at a young age, due to the psychological thought process children have of being perceived different from other children they associate with. In the mindset of most children, to be different, somehow makes you weird or strange. It's not until early adolescence, which is around 9-14 years of age, that children start developing psychological needs to achieve self-dominance and independence. That is when they seek opportunities to demonstrate their new talents and their capacity to control their behavior. They have cognitive changes, where perception becomes realized. Self-realization begins, and the learning of the world outside their family structure. This is also the time where the comparing of development and performance with other peers are realized. This behavior can follow a person the rest of their life, based on how their personal values and self-esteem is perpetuated.

There should be a point in time when you learn to love everything about you. Learn that the areas you fall short in create an understanding that adds to your perfection, and helps you reach your true purpose. Imperfections let the world see your humanity. If you can't love and appreciate you, who actually can? You teach people how to treat you. Perfection is only in the movies and can be hazardous to your health. Living up to someone else's perception or truths about life robs you from being the best you that you can be. Don't confuse perfection with excellence. We should all strive for excellence in whatever we do, but trying to be perfect is a set up for unnecessary stress and let-downs. This psychology goes right along with being concerned with what others think. You can only be an excellent you, and a second rate someone else.

Being concerned with what others think is a form of fear, and fear cause oppression. Being fearful of what others think causes insecurities, and handicaps your forward progress. There are many people who will never reach destiny because popular opinion won't let them. They become catatonic; unable to move and make their own decisions. Fear is not a physicality, it is a mentality that is taught or learned. When you're concerned with what others think, you're displaying a fear that disables your design, your purpose for living.

The American culture has become a place where people feel a sense of entitlement; having the attitude that humanity owes them something, and not them owing humanity. This attitude is causing major set-backs in the development of future generations. What happened to the mindset of your children going further in life than their parents? Your children should be a continuation of who you were here on the earth. It's your job to teach them by example, how to take responsibility for their own circumstances. This requires you to allow your children to experience some type of desperation, which means you can't give them everything they desire. Desperation affords you the wonderful opportunity to dig inside yourself to find those answers that lie within. Some things can only be discovered in those times of deep yearning. In order for your children to become active contributing citizens, this is a must. I have met countless single women that feel that the way you compensate for the absence of the father, is to give their child whatever they desire. This methodology has started an epidemic of children growing up lost and without purpose. These young adults blame their parents for their present state with the attitude that their parents were responsible for their bad choices. They feel as if they were never given any direction or sense of purpose. These same youth are controlled even more by the thoughts of others, because they are desperately searching even harder for acceptance.

Having no sense of direction is the number one reason people are concerned with what others think about them. Anything that you think about often, meditate on, visualize consistently, and focus on, will be the thing you give birth to. It is the law of attraction in operation.

Peer pressure is very real and has caused many tragedies, even fatalities. There should be a great balance between the popular opinion of others and the thoughts and concerns you have about yourself.

If you possess a deep need to have your ideas and thoughts validated by others, there are some insecurity issues that may need addressing. What's wrong with daring to believe in your own ideas and beliefs? Somebody had to dare to go against popular opinion in order for us to have airplanes, and cargo ships that do our importing and exporting. Who are those people that have dared to not accept the status quo and launch out into unchartered waters to find new, innovative ways and ideas to exist.

I challenge you, the reader of this book, to believe in the creativity of your own print (fingerprint). In spite of what the facts of life have tried to show you. Facts are only subject to absolute truth.

What are the facts in your life that a new truth can change? It may be a fact that you have more month than money right now, but the truth is that there is a creative idea in you, that when put into action, will change that fact.

You need a paradigm shift. Dare to be different. Trust your inner-self. Reacquaint yourself with your true self.

It only takes one thought put into action that can take you from the place of not enough to more than enough. Don't be concerned with the thoughts of others concerning your life. Become that person who is known by the gifts you have been courageous enough to display to the world. Popular opinion will never allow you to walk in your gifts and talents. It will only serve to put you in a place of bondage, forever fearful of leaving your contribution to the world.

6

WHY DO WE HAVE TRIBULATIONS?

I overheard someone saying some pretty negative things about me that were not true. The conversation was about my living conditions. The picture was painted as if I was less than a man because I was not employed at the time, and I was living with someone else. They were insinuating that I was living off of someone like a child living off his father.

As I sat and thought about what had taken place, I'm reminded of JESUS' crucifixion…He told GOD the FATHER to forgive those that had defamed HIS name; to forgive those who have condemned HIM to die, even though HE knew it would be unto death. HIS reason was that they "knew not what they do". If they REALLY knew that HE was their SAVIOR they would never have spoken ill of HIM. Another scripture that came to mind was to love and pray for those that persecute you (Matt.5:44Amp); Also, I love this next verse, (Luke 6:27-28 Amp) where HE says "to treat well (do good to, act nobly toward) those who detest you and pursue you with hatred, and pronounce BLESSINGS (GOD FAVOR) upon those who abuse you (who revile, reproach, disparage, and high-handedly misuse you)." WOW, that's POWERFUL! Why in the world would the LORD say these things concerning your enemies? The author asked the question, why should GOD reward you if you only love the people that love you? Basically, are you showing HIM that you're HIS son or daughter if you only pray and wish good for those that do the same for you? Jesus was literally broken and beat to pieces for us to LIVE (not to get what we deserve), so if we are going to reign with HIM we must suffer with him. WE HAVE TO BE BROKEN BREAD AND POURED WINE. We must be food for those that don't know how to feed off of GOD'S WORD yet. Until they are enlightened on how to commune with HIM on their own, it's our duty as believers to be their bridge and feed them (John.21:17). We can never be OVERCOMERS if we never have anything to overcome. We must trust the struggle. Today I was reminded of those struggles; the struggle of unemployment; the struggle of being dependent on others for help; the struggle of fighting the feelings of "why me"; the struggle of what I did to deserve my life circumstances…basically, the classic "poor me syndrome"? This prompted me to look up the word "STRUGGLE". The Webster Dictionary describes struggle as making strenuous or violent efforts in the face of difficulties or opposition; or to proceed with difficulty and great effort. How many of you are struggling today? How many are facing difficult times, opposition or having to use great effort to maintain a positive attitude or outlook on life? I implore you to TRUST YOUR STRUGGLE. I know you all are probably wondering just how you trust something that's difficult and painful. Hmm...it puts me in the mind of an exercise in weight training. Those who are into muscle growth know that you have to tear down your muscles in order for them to GROW. Even though it is a painful, strenuous, and sometimes difficult task, it is a requirement for GROWTH, and as your muscles get familiar with the pain associated with it, it starts to feel differently. So, you might ask, "Are you saying that struggle means GROWTH?" Yes, that's exactly what I'm saying. There are many life experiences where we encounter struggle but we are also building strength.

Physical struggles for muscle growth, or mental struggles, which build CHARACTER and INTEGRITY, are all being strengthened. Spiritually your faith is growing as well. The carnal man on the other hand, is taking a beating; it hates to be told no. As you practice telling your physical man "no", your SPIRIT MAN begins to GROW, and your whole life is affected.

You've heard it said, that it only takes 30 days for something to become a habit (good, bad or indifferent); that is why it is important to get into the practice of repeating affirmations daily. Speak to your situation (tribulations), tell it "thank you", UNDERSTANDING they're EQUIPPING you for GROWTH. (Rom.5:3) The Amplified bible states "moreover (let us also be full of joy now!) let us exalt and triumph in our troubles and rejoice in our sufferings, knowing that pressure and affliction and hardship produce patient and unswerving endurance".

Your mind has the power to take you wherever you want it to go (power of thought). TRUST that your STRUGGLE or tribulations you encounter, will take you just where you want to go and need to be. TRUST THE STRUGGLE to introduce you to your DESTINY and your PROMISE!!! Most people really don't trust the struggle, so they abort and tap out (quit and/or blame others). Will you trust the tribulations in your life and let it have its PERFECT WORK in you? I hope so because it is the only way to be BUILT for the job; the job of a BELIEVER, a TRUE KINGDOM BUILDER.

In life, we all have different experiences or different "crushings", per se, but we all must be broken and crushed to those lustful, material desires and systematic ways of thinking. Our minds have to be renewed daily. I don't know about you but I know I'm right where I'm supposed to be. Your position must be a position of believing yourself worthy of doing the best you can do! Whatever it takes for your growth, you have to be willing to walk that walk and embrace the breaking, knowing that GOD is with you no matter what. Start thanking HIM for the new ideas being birthed out of your crushing and trust your inner-self to show you how to carry them out.

Continue to trust the struggle, which is your carnal man (physical) fighting with your spirit man. Be aware of the world's devices and how it uses the media and television to lock you into a certain way of thinking. Again, all of these reality shows are corrupting the minds of people, including believers in GOD as well. Yes I said believers. I know people that love GOD, but for some strange reason they believe they can watch every demonic, GODLESS and perverted thing on television and feel as though they're exempt from the effects. I'm sorry to inform you, but whatever you take into your mind will play itself out in some form or fashion. I'm not saying you can't watch TV, but you must be mindful of what you're feeding your mind.

Your mind has to be guarded at all times. Even while you're asleep, your mind is still working (unconscious mind), thinking on ideas for the next day or processing things that you feed it that day. Our mind is fed by both the soul and the spirit. We have two things working in us at all times. We have our natural senses (soul) and we also have a GOD man (inner-self). When you constantly feed the mind through soulish behavior, you disable your inner-man to take control. You empower and feed your inner-man by digesting the word of God which gives you a positive understanding of who you truly are and speaking those words of affirmation. This is where the struggle begins, but rest assured the fight has been fixed. Your enemy has already been defeated. As you trust your inner-man roughout the struggle, it will then build you.

Our actions start to become more like the creator (in His likeness), becoming more sensitive concerning the things of our spirit. Trusting the struggle means you trust the lessons that come from the struggle. Trusting the development GOD is allowing, to refine you. GOD has a way of strategically strengthening those things that need to be strengthened and destroying those things that need to be released out of your life. Psalms 66:8-12 in the Message bible states "Bless our GOD, O peoples! Give him a thunderous welcome! Didn't He set us on the road to life? Didn't He keep us out of the ditch? He trained us first, passed us like silver through refining fires, brought us into hardscrabble country, pushed us to our very limit, Road-tested us inside and out, took us to hell and back; Finally He brought us to this well-watered place. Wow, doesn't that sound like the struggles of life? How many of you feel like you have been to hell and back? I'm sure quite a few, but the GLORIOUS thing is that when you come out, the ABUNDANCE of the BLESSING is so great! The pain that was inflicted during the struggle is no longer felt. It is kind of like a natural childbirth. I've heard mothers say the pain of having a child naturally, is beyond description, yet the joy of birthing life is so great, that the pain associated with it can't compare. Don't we serve an amazing GOD?

The next time life happens and GOD allows a storm to come your way, don't forget to remember these three words. Trust your struggle!

7

WHAT DO YOU DO WHILE WAITNG ON YOUR MANIFESTATION

As I awoke on Saturday morning, and worked out with some friends at "Foster Beach" in Chicago, Ill. Yeah, I know, you're wondering how a trip to Chicago happens with no employment, right? Well, GOD is truly amazing!! As I was writing this I was sitting eating breakfast at "Nookies", a nice American style restaurant. The food was great and if you're ever in Chicago's Historic District in Edgewater, you should try it. As I reflect back to that Friday, I'm thanking GOD again for allowing me to TRUST HIM. Initially, I wasn't going to make the trip because of my financial situation. However, I began to ponder "what is it that you do when you're waiting on things to manifest in your life; while you're waiting on doors to open for you?"

Are you waiting on that next great million dollar idea, or waiting on a response to the hundreds of applications for employment you've submitted? Well friends, I say you take advantage of every opportunity and seize every moment. Take advantage of every opportunity to see something new; opportunities to meet someone new;

opportunities to learn something new. It's called networking and that's exactly what I was doing with limited financial means. I've learned that as you become a BLESSING to others, they will be a BLESSING to you, which is a Kingdom principle.

I was asked to help some friends drive back to my old residence, in the city I once lived in. As I called a few people to let them know I was coming to town, one friend, (Matthew B Coleman) asked me to accompany him to Chicago later that evening, and further stated that I need not worry about spending money because he had me covered, not only for me helping him with the drive, but also for providing great company! How many people think you're great company and want you around them for inspiration or simply to have a good time?

We all have qualities that people love about us. Do you know what your qualities are? If so, how are you perfecting them? Do you read? Do you pray? What are the things you're practicing that will help you be a better you? One of the biggest tricks your mind sometimes plays on you is to convince you that you should be alone and isolated. Don't be deceived; there is power in unity. There is power in being connected with others of like minds.

The Bible talks about touching and agreeing with others; (Matt. 18:19-20) those wanting the same things you do. If the bible is correct, which I believe it is, why do we as people run away from others when we're going through life's challenging experiences? Is it embarrassment? Is it that we don't want others to know what we lost; what money or material things we no longer have? Well, I was forced to silently answer each of those questions as I was transitioning to my PROMISE!

Friends, the battle we fight as people, as BELIEVERS in GOD, are in the mind. I found myself wanting to hide from the world out of embarrassment and a fear of being judged. I started to see how the mind will use the ego to shake you. Luke 22:31 reads "Simon, Simon (Peter), listen! Satan has asked excessively that (all of) you be given up to him (out of the power and keeping of GOD), that he might sift (all of) you like grain. What this means is that your mind, when given into your lower-self, will actually give you permission to play mind games with yourself. The sad thing is, most people don't understand this trick and fall prey to every device that is used to hinder your progress. It should not matter to you what others think about your position in life and if they really even care.

As I'm starting to understand the POWER and AUTHORITY I walk in, I am not ashamed of where I was in life. I know the valley is all for the greater good. It has prepared me for where I'm going. I understand that it's WHAT WE DO while waiting on our manifestation that truly determines if and how fast we come through the trials of life.

The children of Israel could have made it through the wilderness in one week, but it took them 40 years to get to their PROMISE LAND. It took the dying away of the old mindsets for them to get their INHERITANCE. The old mindset was the Red Sea mindset. The Red Sea mindset waited to see circumstances change first, however, GOD was now trying to get them to first BELIEVE HIS PROMISE, then HE would move in their favor. It took the dying off of the older generation who needed a sign to believe. The children that INHERITED THE PROMISED LAND were the ones that TRULY BELIEVED their needs were already taken care of.

So friends, as you transition into your PROMISE, don't be fooled by your circumstances and tuck yourself away or isolate yourself from the world. Get out with others and enjoy every moment. Do things you couldn't do before, due to your work schedule and other obligations. Surround yourself with like-minded people that believe in your dreams; those who BELIEVE your promise is closer than you think. Our GOD is not a respecter of person. If HE did it for Moses, HE WILL DO IT FOR YOU! He esteems no one higher or better than the other.

I was sent something to read by a friend and it was labeled "Down Time". The author challenged you to examine the time(s) in your own life, you deemed unproductive. This time of being unproductive was referred to as "DOWN TIME". The author further challenges us to begin thinking of "DOWN TIME" as a season where GOD is allowing certain situations and events to take place in your life so that you can grow, develop, and be stretched, if you will. This growth spurt can catapult you into the right position to MAXIMIZE your potential. Therefore, when you take a closer look, your lack of productivity may not be unproductive at all.

A few months ago, I told a friend that there are times when you need to "REST" before you move into your next phase. I further stated that we, as a society, are so used to being busy that we view REST as being lazy. In actuality, REST is a time of mental PREPARATION, a time for REFLECTION. REST keeps you from becoming tired or jaded, and can erase the deemed failures of the prior year or season from your memory. REST, or as we are referring to it, "DOWN TIME" is a CLEANSING!

Many people never realize or even think about the benefits of "DOWN TIME". However, during the winter months, gardeners must WAIT until that season has expired to plant seeds. The winter months are very important for gardening. The winter freeze improves the soil and also lightens it up. The snow insulates plants that would otherwise never survive the low temperatures. The cold keeps pests and diseases under control. Now picture that from a human life perspective. GOD has always used nature to give us understanding of how HE wants us to operate. How many of us embrace the winter season; that time of stillness or WAITING?

Let's talk about Stress for a moment. Stress is one of the top killers of mankind. Why is this so? Stress opens up your body to all kind of health issues that can be fatal. About two years ago, I found myself not embracing my time of WAITING. I started to allow all the "what if's" to stress me out. My body started to break out into hives and I would itch all over. The thing is, most of what I allowed to stress me out, were things I could not do anything about, I just needed to WAIT. I needed to allow certain things to play out in my life. This makes me reflect back to another time in my life when I started my business and unfortunately, my business partner was not fulfilling their obligation in the partnership. The situation placed such extreme pressure and stress upon me, that for the first time in my life, I found myself in the hospital for a stress condition. I had no concept of what stress could put your body through. Mind you, at that time, I was only 28 years of age. I couldn't believe I was experiencing this condition, (stress) again. I did the only thing I knew to do and that was ask GOD (inner-self), what should I be doing? GOD continued to tell me to look within. As the situation worsened, I decided to just embrace it in spite of it all and enjoy life, for after all, there was nothing I could do but WAIT. I found myself on a real vacation; a vacation from my problems, laughing out loud. As I embraced my "DOWN TIME", I found that many of the problems I thought I had were really not problems at all, but rather GOD'S way of telling me that it was time for something new.

A major overhaul was in the making. HE was erasing memories of failures of the year before, scouring my mental landscape. I was and still am being pruned and cleared of anything superfluous or undesirable; pruned from toxic people, pruned from old mindsets and self-destructive behavior. I knew that when I came out of that season there would be no weeds, no drought, and no personal idiocies. My life was being freed from impurities. My load had been lightened and I was insulated to survive the lows in my life.

Those who know me know that I'm a giver of LIGHT and ENERGY, and that nothing can hold me for long, because I BELIEVE in the power of my print. True BELIEVERS understand that their way is already paved. Your job is to weather the storm; to embrace life's lessons and testify of our GOD'S GOODNESS and MAJESTY to others.

8

HOW DO YOU CONQUER FEAR

Fear is an enemy of your HEART'S DESIRES. Fear will rob you from the greatest things GOD intends for you to have. You have to check fear or it will turn into panic. The Bible says "fear hath torment" (1John 4:18 KJV). You have to open your mouth and talk back to fear. Speak The WORD... Speak! For GOD did not give us the spirit of timidity (fear) but of POWER, LOVE, CALM, WELL- BALANCED, DISCIPLINE, SELF-CONTROL, and a SOUND MIND (2Tim 1:7)!!! You have to tell fear you don't have time for it! NOW, LATER or EVER! Fear will talk you out of things (DESTINY) you have been given permission to have.

You PRAY for things and GOD grants it, but because it is not totally packaged just right or may take a little more patience to fully manifest, you get scared and run. You can't look at where you are and what you have to sum up what you think you're capable of doing. There are hidden resources that you have no idea exist, and destiny is just waiting for the right ingredient (FAITH) to release it.
There are strengths that have been put inside you to weather any storm. Why seek the opinions of others

and try to figure out how and what to do in moments of fear? The world can never tell you what destiny has already said you can have. They can never tell you the potential you possess. If GOD said you can have it, it's yours!
HE has already made you wealthy, you just have to take hold of your wealth.

Understand that you will be tested on everything you believe. It's the job of the powers that be, to try and make you run away and forfeit your blessing. Trials of life will try and scare you from moving when your inner-self say's go! There will always be provision for what your inner-self tells you to do and where HE tells you to go. You may not always feel it or see it, but you must believe it! That's the hardest thing for people to do, is BELIEVE they can be or have their hearts desires. The fights you fight through qualify you for things to come. Don't despise the struggle or battle you are in. Whatever challenges or fears that may attack you, please be reminded that you are right where you are supposed to be! Keep the right spirit and fight for what's yours. GOD is looking for the people HE can trust with their hearts desires; those who won't run from their promises, those that can believe and tell fear to back off! Any time you go to the bottom and you're raised back up, you don't have to be worried about becoming arrogant and self-consumed. You can be trusted with the promises you were born to bless the world with. With one look back, you are reminded of how far you have come.

GOD is looking for people who remember what HE has protected them from, and what HE has placed inside you even when you didn't believe and fully trust it. What fear has you running and forfeiting your GOD given rights and promises? I challenge you to HAVE FAITH and BELIEVE what's inside of you.

GOD is not a man that he would lie or tempt you with something only to then have you become fearful of it. Believe in the promises inside and watch your hearts desires manifest

9

HOW DO YOU FIND PURPOSE?

Proverbs 19:12 in the amplified bible states, "Many plans are in a man's mind, but it is the LORD'S PURPOSE for him that will stand".
You were designed for a certain PURPOSE. You may not know it, but it doesn't change what you were designed to do. GOD might allow different situations and circumstances to come into our lives that may confuse or change what our PURPOSE looks like, but HE will never change your PURPOSE. PURPOSE is so serious that Jesus made an example of a fig tree. The fig tree was alive yet bearing no fruit. Jesus cursed the fig tree and it dried it up for not producing fruit, (Mark.11;12-13) to serve as an example as to how important fulfilling our purpose is. Our true PURPOSE is what gives us meaning. Jesus cursed the fig tree for not operating in its PURPOSE for existing. Your vocation or occupation is most likely not your PURPOSE but may be the vehicle or training used to get you there.

There are many people that are so consumed with their jobs that they miss their intended PURPOSE. The most confusing part is that most don't even like their job; they actually loathe going there, but continue to do so for that all mighty dollar.

Jesus' profession was a carpenter (Mark.6:3), but that wasn't HIS PURPOSE. Jesus' PURPOSE was to fulfill a new Will and Testament. He came to fulfill the law. He died as a ransom for our sins. HIS PURPOSE was to give us GRACE (unmerited favor).

Think with me for a moment.....

What if HE hadn't fulfilled HIS PURPOSE? Where would you and I be? How difficult would life really be?
What if I hadn't left Ohio and "transitioned" to Georgia, in obedience to that inner voice? The fact of the matter is that Believers should be more concerned about being obedient to that voice than about how much money you make because PURPOSE is the only thing that completes you. Yes, I know we need our jobs to pay our bills and to take care of our families, I get that!, BUT... Think of something small, like a belt you wear in your pants. What if it didn't operate in its PURPOSE. We would all have to get super tight fitted pants and shorts (laugh out loud), to compensate for what a belt could have done. Let's take a pair of socks. If we didn't wear socks, our feet would not be protected from sweating too

much while wearing shoes, or from getting too cold from the cold weather, or from blisters that would form because of the sensitivity of our feet. This may seem a little silly but it is very true. Everything has a purpose and if it does not operate in its PURPOSE, it is in total violation of the reason it was made. Without PURPOSE we are reckless and lifeless.

Think about the absence of fathers that have crippled the human race. I know so many boys, girls, and even adult men and women who are dealing with scars based on the absence of their fathers not operating in their role or PURPOSE.
One of the jobs of a father is to impart PURPOSE, which gives direction in the lives of their children. Every father should have a plan for his family; a road map if you will, to a destination he has planned for them to be by a certain time. Daughters should learn how to love by the way their fathers love them. A young man should learn how to love a woman based on his father's love for his mother.
Fathers, being the head or protectors of the house, should also impart PURPOSE in their children. Their PURPOSE should come from daddy. Some would dare to say that this is the job of their teacher but it is not the teacher's job to see the greatness in your children.

Teachers have your sons and daughters eight hours a day, Monday through Friday, for eight months out of the year. How does that make it their job to motivate, encourage and speak PURPOSE into the life of your child? Let me help you. It isn't. Their job is to educate, whether it's basic A, B, C's or teaching them physics. Teachers should have the awesome job of simply reinforcing the positive teachings instilled at home and should be able to push children in the PURPOSE that has already been realized from the parent GOD has established for them.

I know you're probably thinking, "that's not the world we live in today" (but it should be). We live in a society today, that has taken the influence of the father and exchanged it for media propaganda, which has given a false and or superficial since of PURPOSE. Our boys, girls, women, and men are now being influenced and educated by TV, movies and tabloids of the latest celebrity love triangles. This is a serious issue with America and the world. We are dying as a culture due to the lack of fathers walking in their PURPOSE. If your father never spoke purpose into you as a child, it does not negate your true self. You may have a more difficult route, but if you seek to know, God will allow someone to come into your life and point you to the Truth. You will then be able to speak PURPOSE into the lives of your own children. Not knowing your PURPOSE is a true tragedy and is passed down from generation to generation.

How many women do you know who live with men that they are not married to or even engaged to? That is not walking in GODS PURPOSE. GOD never designed a man and a woman to live together outside of the sanctity of marriage. This is how couples get trapped trying to take the "easy route". Most times, women feel it is the job of the man to take care of her, which is not true until he marries her. The "easy route", meaning living together to split the bills or whatever, is where the trap begins to form. Number one, if the man is paying all the bills and the women isn't saving her money and they are not married, where is her security? If this man never marries her and wants her out his place, then what? Usually there is no money saved for her to get a place of her own, and she has accumulated debt. She has a big problem now because she has nowhere to go, and GOD forbid if there is a child involved.

The flip side is also true. Most men trap women on purpose, knowing once she's trapped with nowhere to go, he has total control. Then the real abuse starts. HE starts to break her down, by cheating, threatening, and calling her out of her name. These women are sometimes beaten and verbally assaulted as well. With the woman feeling embarrassed or alone, she will usually stay in the relationship for years before mustering up enough strength to leave. By this time she could be well up in age with severe psychological issues that could take years to repair. Either way, her self-worth begins to be depleted. You might be thinking how does this cycle continue? It continues because the generation before them have never broken the cycle and sometimes even encouraged the same sick thinking to the son or daughter. It bothers me to see women encouraging their daughters to live with their boyfriends so that they may be taken care of.

Young ladies, take care of yourself until GOD decides to bless you with your true life partner (HUSBAND).

Trust that what you have inside you is enough to take care of you. You will do a much better job than any man ever can. Stay in your GOD given PURPOSE. Wait on that qualified man who's being developed and specially designed for you. When he comes, he will love you too much to insult you with the idea of buying the milk before the cow (shacking) and playing married. You will know him when he comes, because he will be in the image and likeness of what you truly yearn for inside.

Know your worth! Your worth does not stem from a man taking care of you or paying your bills, but in GODS PURPOSE for your life. The things that GOD PURPOSED for you will line up with what is inside of you. PURPOSE would never call for a man and woman to play house and take the easy or convenient route. When a women and a man come together, they should add to and complement each other, making whatever you were doing apart, greater. That's GODS PURPOSE for your life, two whole people coming together, becoming greater.

If some of you women would be honest, you would say that at one time you really believed your PURPOSE was to serve and please your man. I know many battered, confused and scarred women that have never recovered from such thinking. They feel they have already given the best of themselves away. Let's kill this stinking thinking and look within. GOD has already placed inside you what you need to win. Your job is to listen to that inner voice and watch your PURPOSE unfold. It's never too late to do a new thing in your life and start on the road of PURPOSE.

So what do you do when your natural father has never spoken PURPOSE into your life, and has never really showed you how to love or be loved by example?

To understand the function or PURPOSE of something, you go to the manufacturer or maker of the thing. GOD is our marker, so you must learn how to read the instructions and meditate on the blueprint your creator left you. It's in the world's best-selling book of all times. I believe the Bible stands for Basic Instructions Before Leaving Earth.

The Bible is the true personal growth and self-development manual. It takes a mature person to accept the teachings this book has to offer. It explains JESUS' PURPOSE and the benefits it has afforded us to those who believe. You will learn the PURPOSE of the HOLY SPIRIT, and HIS job to guide you into all truth (JOHN 16:13). This book has taught me that speaking its words will cause manifestation; that out of the abundance of the heart is where a man speaks.

Many people are busy doing all kinds of things that may or may not be self-fulfilling, but are not on the path to PURPOSE. Remember, no matter how much we resist or fight to go another route, our PURPOSE never changes. Don't forget the story of Jonah. (Jonah 1:2) Jonah ran as long as he could from his assignment (PURPOSE). His disobedience caused issues for others. On your way to PURPOSE, others will be affected if you refuse to walk in your design. As Jonah was sleeping on the ship, on his way to Tarshish, which was not a part of his PURPOSE, a storm hit the ship causing the others to have great fear. When they woke Jonah up he was quite clear on why the storm had arose and told the men to throw him over board, where he was then swallowed by a big fish (Whale) for 3 days and 3 nights. Yes, we jeopardize other people when we do not walk in our PURPOSE, but at the end of the day GOD'S PURPOSE never changed.

Jonah went through, and put others through, unnecessary turmoil for not following GOD'S plan for his life. How many times have you done things you knew you weren't supposed to do, affecting others, just to end up doing it anyway? Jonah was given detailed instructions. He knew what his assignment was BEFORE his PURPOSE was revealed. His running away just delayed his PURPOSE being revealed. One way or another, GOD'S plan will be done when listening to your inner-self. After suffering and experiencing a life changing event, Jonah was happy to be obedient! His obedience (like mine) became apparent as he walked in that inner knowing.

How many of you are in self-inflicted turmoil, for not following or understanding your PURPOSE? How many are sad, depressed, and empty, going through the motions of life pretending to have joy and peace, running from that small voice (inner-self). GOD is whispering in your ear, telling you not to be afraid and be in good courage and walk out in faith and do those things you know to do. Just like HE did with Jonah, GOD has a way of redirecting you. Whether, HE allows pain or misfortune, to come on you because of disobedience or ignorance, you still have a choice. A choice to have true peace, joy and fulfillment by following HIS plan. You must do what GOD has placed inside you and stay on the path of PURPOSE.

When I left Ohio in obedience to GOD (my inner-voice), I was following my PURPOSE; the calling GOD had on my life. I didn't know all the details of my transition nor do I now, but what I do know is that HE has provided provision for every step of the way. With that being said, I received a source of income, after eight months of living without (trusting my inner-voice). I've been having the time of my life. I have had some bumps and bruises; wounds, and tremendous heart break, but I'm still here trusting and living from the inside out. When you trust what GOD has placed inside you, valleys feel like mountain tops.

Break the cycle and be transformed by the renewing of your mind, so you may prove what's good, acceptable and perfect in GODS will for your life (Romans 12:2

10

HOW DO YOU TAKE ACTION?

As I sit here in a place I never knew existed a year and a half ago, enjoying the sunshine and feeling the spring breeze, I'm reminded of how glorious life can be with all of the beautiful, amazing aspects of being healthy and aware of my humanity. I have been enlightened to the truths of what to expect and what I should be striving for. I've been blessed to understand my true rights as a Follower of Christ. Our creator has given us everything we need to win "sweatlessly" .

How do you know when you're winning Sweatlessly? This realization occurs when you start viewing your failures the same as you do your victories.

Even when you fail you're winning because it gives you the opportunity to learn what not to do (what doesn't work). Your mind has the incredible power to receive things spoken from within. When you speak that you're a winner, everything in the Universe starts working on your behalf to bring what you spoke to pass. Scientists have been baffled for centuries, trying to figure out and make mathematical sense concerning the powers of spoken words. Man has the capability to speak whatever he want into existence. Your thoughts will shape your situation. They will direct your actions, determine the opportunities that come your way, and affect the outcome of the things you attempt. If you want to change your standing, you must change your thoughts. You must put into action your purpose, leaving distractions powerless. To understand your design, fingerprint, and WHY for being, is to be liberated and set free. It's absolute freedom out of bondage (restrictions). It is the beginning of self-realization and ultimate empowerment!

Life is filled with choices, and those choices should be made based on certain outcomes you plan to have. These choices will help you raise up a standard of what you will and will not do. Most people will make long-term decisions in temporary situations, which can cause a huge problem when that season of your life has passed and the decision you made in that season follows you into the next, causing unnecessary pressure. This could be relational or financial. The goals you set for yourself will help you to set boundaries that will determine the things you won't do. This a very important thought because boundaries not kept can destroy careers and break up relationships. When setting goals, you are laying a road map to a destination that will help you to focus on the right types of friends and associates you need and should accept. It also gives understanding of time frames, which can slow down procrastination.

I believe all people have the capacity to lead, and should lead in something. How do you lead? A leader gives guidance. A leader gives instruction. A leader also has to go before whatever or whomever they are leading. What I'm saying is, a leader must be trained and developed in order to lead. What does that mean? Glad you asked (smiles). A leader must pave the way! Often times he or she must tread in foreign waters first. They may have to go through unchartered territory first. By following specialized instructions and practice, a leader is developed. In order to lead people, one must become proficient in their field. Pain is a necessary feeling for the development of a leader that is walking after purpose.

Jesus, being a perfect illustration, bore every pain associated with this world. HE faced abandonment, frustration, loneliness, and betrayal, which leads me to believe that there must be a process to this thing called leadership. For those of you who know that you have been called to lead, don't focus on the process, focus on the understanding that GOD has made you a promise that HE is with you now and until the end of time. You may ask, "just what does that mean?" The promise of GOD never leaving or forsaking you means success, favor, and grace; (getting things you didn't earn or deserve); HIS supernatural increase, restoration, honor, increased assets, recognition, and prominence.

Remember the Tortoise and the Hare. It doesn't always matter how fast you start out, but how you finish the race. You must be able to endure until the end. The trials and tribulations you face are HIS way of letting you develop your spiritual muscles. People won't be capable of understanding who you were created to be until that day arrives because they don't possess the capacity to see beyond where they see themselves. People love to put you in the same box they are in. They don't have enough courage to trust the inner- voice for themselves, so they will tell you your faith is silly faith or emotional faith. Again, this is why the closest people to you are so important. You should never tell a person their dream is never reachable, or can't be obtained by the way their inner-voice has led them. Reason being, you are not their god and there are many ways to get to the same destination.
I'm very effective in what I do for a living now and even with past platforms I've had, but my practice and delivery have always been uncommon, unorthodox and not so politically correct. This is okay as long as you're effective and successful at what you do, without breaking any laws and hurting others. That's your gift; your fingerprint that is being showcased the way in which GOD planned

for you to use it. Those people that feel you have to do it their way, are usually masking their own insecurities. They need other people to validate the way they think. So they pressure others to do what they do, so they can feel some form of validation for their actions. It bewilders me why so many people are waiting on GOD to do something for them, when the greatest work HE has already done; the work HE has done in you. Personal growth and self-development books will sometimes trigger that inner-man to come alive. I suggest you read, read, and when you have finished, read some more. There is no age or gender that should stop you from expanding your knowledge. You are what you eat. Whether it's the type of food you eat, the television shows you watch, or the books you read. Everything taken into your body, conscious and unconscious mind, has an effect, and has the power to shape and form you mentally and physically. Pay attention to how you treat the gift GOD gave you. As I get older, I'm much more conscious of the things I subject my mind, body, and soul to. I am much more aware of the damage that could be inflicted on me if I allow certain things and people access to me.

Guarding your fingerprint is a day to day process, and will take a lot of will power on any given day because the reaching power of negativity and media influence is all around us. This reminds me of conversations in the Bible, that talk about believers in Christ being not conformed to this world's way of thinking and doing things. Even in biblical times there were issues with people being influenced by negativity and religious doctrine that hindered the masses from walking in their design.

To move forward in life or your career, you must first accept responsibility for where you're at, without blaming others or waiting for them to show you how. Hopeless situations are only based on what you believe and how you respond. You must continue to weigh the sum total of every decision you make when you're walking in your design or you will be in jeopardy of never acting out that realization. Whatever you consider the most, gives opportunity for it to become a reality and your response is what determines the outcome of it!
Prioritizing is another function that helps you move into action. How do you prioritize when life seems to keep disappointing you? When people come in your life and take a piece of you and leave you all alone? How do you redirect the pain of loss; things you thought would be forever and only lasted for a season? I say you start making choices that fulfill your purpose and destiny.

Life is filled with so many distractions and people without vision and understanding of their purpose, that if you are not careful, they can make your life seem just as empty. Jesus made His decisions based on His purpose. The purpose HE came to fulfill here on earth. HE was never moved or surprised when others turned their back and denied HIM or left HIM. Most people are only consumed with self (their issues and problems), not realizing that when you help others GOD is obligated to help you. Remember to focus on your goals you have set and not the problems of life. When you understand your purpose, you know why people do what they do, or why your finances may not be where you want them, as well as any other situation that plagues your life. So when people leave you or deceive you and hurt you. Don't let the pain take you out of the race. Truthfully they are the ones really hurting. It's not for you to dislike them or talk negatively about them, but to pray that God enlightens them to HIS purpose.

When people are purpose driven, they look at life with a different pair of lenses. Money, relationships, and past scares never affect or stop them from their purpose, so let purpose (vision) be the guide that leads you to those people you let into your heart. The Bible says that people perish for the lack of knowledge (vision) which is attached to your purpose. You never want to give the wrong people too much of your time and emotions. It could delay or derail you from your purpose. So as you make your life plan to deal with the challenges of this world, make sure you allow GOD'S (that inner-voice) purpose to determine your priorities.

As I sum up this book, I would like to press upon you that success, great wealth, and living life with SWEATLESS VICTORIES is not a secret formula, but a way of thinking and being. You have to be purposeful in your behavior and actions in order to walk out your design, purpose, and your why for living. You have already started your walk of self-discovery by reading this book. Congratulations and welcome to the first day of the rest of your life. Be encouraged! Be courageous and empowered to walk in your own space and cut out your own path without the influence of the media, TV, or popular opinion, but by your inner-man's voice(the GOD in you).

11

AFFIRMATIONS

To command the finish works of Jesus, we as believers must audibly speak what GOD speaks. When the WORD of GOD is spoken in the name of JESUS, HIS WORD starts to take root and come alive in you. Jesus consistently stated that HE only spoke what he heard HIS father speak. Like Jesus, we must speak what HE speaks. This is GOD'S will.

There are AFFIRMATIONS I have been confessing during my "TRANSITION". Some of these affirmations I have been confessing for over 15 years. As you read and speak GOD'S word into the atmosphere, let it take root and believe you already receive the finished works of Jesus Christ. Remember, this was paid for you already by the blood that Jesus shed on Calvary. These are our blood bought rights and privileges.

"Father, in the name of Jesus. I thank you that the set time for favor on my life is now! "I choose to walk in the favor of GOD in every area of my life. I am the righteousness of GOD because of what Jesus did for me on Calvary, therefore favor surrounds me as shield."

"I thank you, FATHER for your WORD that declares that the favor of GOD on my life will cause promotion and increase according to Genesis 39:21-23."

"I believe I am experiencing supernatural promotion and increase in every area of my life."

"I thank you, FATHER, for increase in real estate acquisitions according to Deuteronomy 33:23 and Psalms 44:3."

"FATHER, I thank you that because of the supernatural favor on my life and family's lives we are delivered out of conflict and dispute according to Joshua 6:22-24."

"FATHER, I thank you that according to 1 Samuel 16:22, favor brings prominence, allowing me to be brought into places that others would marvel."

"I release my faith for genuine friendships and I release my faith to be a godly example in their lives."

"I thank you FATHER, for favor that causes preferential treatment according to Ruth 2:12-16."

"You cause others to go out of their way to cater unto me."

"Thank you Father, that favor causes petitions to be granted from hostile authority according to Exodus 3:21-22."

"Therefore, every person that you have spoken to concerning blessing me and my family is released to follow through on what you have spoken to them to do."

"I thank you FATHER, that favor causes policies to be reversed according to Esther 8:4-8."

"Therefore, you are raising up somebody to reverse the policy for me. I understand that it is through praise that I accelerate the favor of GOD in my life, so I honor you FATHER GOD and worship you."

"I praise you for you alone are worthy of all praise, honor, and glory."

"Thank you FATHER, for there is none like you."

"As your child, I have a right to come boldly before your throne of Grace and find mercy and Grace (unmerited Favor) just when I need it."

"In Jesus name, I thank you FATHER, for the SUPERNATURAL FAVOR on my life NOW, in Jesus name. Amen..!!"

Lord, bless me and keep your face to shine upon me and be gracious unto me. LORD, lift up your countenance upon me, and give me peace (Numbers 6:24-26).

Make me as Ephraim (fruitful) and Manasseh (forgetting my pain) (Genesis 48:20).

Let me be satisfied with favor and be filled with your blessing (Deuteronomy 33:23).

Give me revelation, and let me be blessed (Matthew 16:17).

Let your showers of blessings be upon my life (Ezekiel 34:26).

Let your blessings make me rich (Proverbs 10:22).

Let all nations call me blessed (Malachi 3:12).

Let all generations call me blessed (Luke 1:48).

I am the son of the blessed (Mark 14:61).

I live in the Kingdom of the blessed (Mark 11:10).

My sins are forgiven and I am blessed (Romans 4:7).

Lord, you daily load me with benefits (Psalm 68:19).

I am chosen by GOD and I am blessed (Psalm 65:4).

My seed is blessed (Psalm 37:26).

Let me inherit the land (Psalm 37:22).

I am part of the holy nation and I am blessed (Psalm 33:12).

Lord, bless my latter end, greater than my former (job 42:12).

Lord bless me and cause your face to shine upon me that your way may be known upon the earth, and your saving health among all nations. Let my land yield increase and let the ends of the earth fear you (Psalm 67:1).

I know you favor me because my enemies do not triumph over me (Psalms 41:11).

Lord, be favorable unto my land (Psalm 85:1.)

Let You cause my horn to be exalted (Psalm 89:17).

Lord, this is my set time for favor (Palm 102:13).

Lord, entreat your favor with my whole heart (Psalm 119:58).

Let your favor be upon my life as a cloud of the Latter Rain (Proverbs 16:15).

I am highly favored (Luke 1:28).

I believe in the prophets and I prosper (2 Chronicles 20:20).

I am your servant, Lord prosper me (Nehemiah 2:20).

I live in the prosperity of the king (Jeremiah 23:5).

Lord, you have called me and you will make my way prosperous (Isaiah 48:15).

I pray in secret and you reward me openly (Matthew 6:6).

I fast in secret and you reward me openly (Matthew 6:18).

You reward me because I diligently seek you (Hebrew 11:6).

God you have allowed us to be trampled on, insulted, even made a slave, that we may be brought out into a place of abundance (Psalm 66:12).

I give and it is given to me pressed down, shaken together and running over, shall men give unto my bosom (Luke 6:38).

Open the floodgates of Heaven over my life and I receive more than I have room enough to receive (Malachi 3:10).

Let every hole in my bag be closed in the name of Jesus (Haggai 1:6).

All nations will call me blessed and I will be a delightful land (Malachi 3:12).

I break all curses of poverty, lack, debt, and failure

in the name of Jesus (Matthew 6:33).

Lord, teach me to profit and lead me in the way I should go (Isaiah 48:17).

Let peace be within my walls and prosperity within my palace (Psalm 122:7).

No harm or disaster can befall those who have made the Lord their refuge (shelter from danger) (Psalms 91:10).

ABOUT THE AUTHOR

Lawrence D Tribble Jr., is a GOD-fearing, dedicated, and results-driven Community Leader, Youth advocate, Life & Empowerment Coach, and Author. Lawrence has over 18 years of experience with driving change in communities. His focus revolves around discipline, goal setting, integrated focus on academics, community engagement, volunteer services, along with motivating and empowering diverse groups of youth, families, and individuals. An expert in networking, relationship building, and establishing partnerships with various local and national organizations, Lawrence has proven his ability to successfully develop, initiate, promote, implement and maintain, large-scale, creative, community-based programs and initiatives that incorporate inspired ideas, innovative solutions and advance the core values of respect, responsibility, caring, honesty and faith, thereby leading to improved/enhanced learning which translates to stronger families and healthier communities.

If you would like to follow Lawrence and continue to be empowered, you can visit him @www.lifecoachingwithlawrencetribble.com

www.ingramcontent.com/pod-product-compliance
Lightning Source LLC
Chambersburg PA
CBHW032130090426
42743CB00007B/544